REJOICE THROUGH PROBLEMS

13 STEPS TO VICTORY

Devotional for Use with
The Power to Rejoice: 21 Days to Victory Over your Problems

VERNON L. WILLIAMS, M.S.

Author of *The Power to Rejoice: 21 Days to Victory Over your Problems*

Empowerment Publishers
Columbia, Maryland

Library of Congress Cataloging-in-Publication Data

Williams, Vernon L

Rejoice through Problems: 13 Steps to Victory/Vernon L. Williams

Includes bibliographical references and index.

ISBN 0-9777338-9-0

Published by Empowerment Publishers.

This book is available at quantity discounts with bulk purchase. For more information, please call 866-850-3354.

Do not miss these other top-selling books by Vernon L. Williams

» The Power to Rejoice: 21 Days to Victory Over Your Problems

» Paddle Your Own Boat: 10 Rules that Guarantee Career Success

» 425 Ways to Stretch Your $$$$

» 3 Rules that Guarantee Financial Success

» Why Employees Fail to Meet Performance Expectations & How to Fix the Problem

Available at www.vernonlwilliams.com

Acknowledgments

I wish to thank Michael Moore for giving me the idea to write this devotional as a companion to my book, *The Power to Rejoice: 21 Days to Victory over Your Problems.*

Thanks to Vick LeBlanc for suggestions on the manuscript.

Thanks to Lynne Karanfil for manuscript suggestions, proofreading and for being a sounding board.

Contents

Introduction

Welcome!

I am so excited that you have decided to participate in this life-changing devotional. This is a transformational study to give you actionable wisdom to help you live every moment with joy, even as you encounter problems.

However, living every moment with joy does not stop with you. As Pastor Ken Pierpont said, "The best evidence of the existence of Jesus is the joy in His followers." Nonbelievers will see your joy despite problems and will ask why you can have such an attitude. That opens the door for sharing the reason for your joy - Jesus Christ.

This devotional is a thirteen week, application-oriented Bible study which is broken down as follows:

Week 1 Expect Problems

Week 2 Distinguish between Happiness and Joy

Week 3 Acknowledge that you direct your Emotions

Week 4 Decide to Rejoice

Week 5 Challenge and Replace Joy-Robbing Thoughts

Week 6 Act Based on What you know

Week 7 Focus on the Benefits of Problems

Week 8 Make Gratitude a Habit

Week 9 Create an Obsession for Praying

Week 10 Develop an Eternal Perspective

Week 11 Use Paul as a Role Model

Week 12 Serve Others

Week 13 Keep your Eyes Fixed on Jesus

Each weekly lesson contains daily homework consisting of discussion questions, multiple choice questions, yes/no questions and fill in the blank statements. You should be able to complete the daily homework within thirty minutes.

The devotional is intended to be used in conjunction with my popular book, *The Power to Rejoice: 21 Days to Victory Over Your Problems.*

What qualifies me to write this book?

Having been a follower of Jesus Christ for more than thirty years, I completed a year-long program of intensive study of Biblical counseling and Bible study methods under the direction of Pastor Brent T. Brooks, a graduate of the Dallas Theological Seminary and the founding pastor of Grace Community Church. I have led multiple small group Bible studies, performed one-on-one coaching and led hundreds of seminars.

I have a master's degree in Applied Behavioral Science from Johns Hopkins University.

Beyond that, I have experienced problems. I was passed over for promotion. I was laid off from my job two years before retirement. I was my wife's caregiver for 12 years. After 34 years of marriage, she went to be with the Lord. I have had business setbacks, dealt with financial challenges and relational conflicts. One brother was killed in combat, another died of a heart attack at age 37, still another brother committed suicide, just to name a few of the problems I have faced.

Applying the steps outlined in this study has enabled me to rejoice through these problems.

Best wishes to you as you embark upon this study.

Vernon L. Williams
Columbia, MD
September, 2016

Note: Unless otherwise noted, all scripture verses are taken from the New King James Version.

Week

1

Expect Problems

Focal Verse

*These things I have spoken to you, that in
Me you may have peace. In the world you
will have tribulation; but be of good cheer, I
have overcome the world. (John 16:33)*

Beth and Ryan had been married for nine years. They, and their two young sons, lived in a quiet suburban neighborhood and were regular attendees at a local church. They seemed to be living the American dream. Then, everything changed. Ryan informed Beth that he had fallen in love with another woman and that he wanted a divorce.

It would be an understatement to say that Beth was devastated. "How can this be happening to me", she asked. She continued by saying "I don't deserve this, "I have been a loving and supportive wife" and "marriage should last forever". Even though she had read the statistics that fifty percent of marriages end in divorce, she never expected that it could possibly happen to her.

Beth is an example of someone who has fallen into an all-too-familiar trap – expecting a trouble-free, comfortable life. While this is a noble desire, it simply does not match the Bible. Paul, Job, David, Isaiah, Jeremiah, John the Baptist, James, Peter and John are just few of examples of Biblical people who did not experience a trouble-free life.

Speaking to His disciples, Jesus very bluntly said: "These things I have spoken to you, that in Me you may have peace. In the world you will have tribulation (trouble)." (John 16:33)

Fortunately, Jesus did not stop with His prediction of troubles. He went on to give His disciples (and us) hope by saying, "But be of good cheer, I have overcome the world."

There are three categories of troubles: ones that you just came out of, ones you are in right now, ones that you will be going into. You can experience joy despite those problems. The first step is having realistic expectations.

Questions for discussion, reflection and application

1. The initial reaction most Christians have to problems is shock – "I can't believe this is happening to me." Do you agree? Why or why not?

_____

_____

_____

2. Read John 16:33.

   a. What was Jesus' warning?

_____

_____

_____

   b. Why did Jesus say "You will have trouble" instead of "You might have trouble"?

_____

_____

_____

c. Explain the phrase "In Me you may have peace."

_____

_____

_____

d. What did Jesus tell His disciples to do despite trouble?

_____

_____

_____

e. Why did He tell them to do that?

_____

_____

_____

f. Explain the phrase "I have overcome the world"?

_____

_____

_____

g. How does this verse impact your expectations of problems?

_____

_____

_____

3. A problem-free life is a myth of earth, but a reality in heaven. Do you agree? Why or why not?

_____

_____

_____

4. Parents are not supposed to bury children; it should be the other way around. Does this statement match the Bible? Why or why not?

_____

_____

_____

Day 2

1. If you are a "good person", i.e. attend church, pray regularly, give to worthwhile causes, serve others, take care of your family, and are loyal to your spouse, you do not deserve to experience accidents, illness, job layoffs, broken relationships, financial setbacks, family strife, death of loved ones and any other kind of problems that unbelievers experience.

a. Do you agree with this point of view? Why or why not?

_____

_____

_____

b. Is this point of view held by many Christians?

_____

_____

_____

c. Does this point of view match John 16:33?

_____

_____

_____

2. If you have enough faith you will not have problems. Do you agree? Why or why not?

_____

_____

_____

3. Read Job 14:1 and 1 Thessalonians 3:3. Do the verses match or contradict John 16:33?

_____

_____

_____

4. Read Psalm 34:19. What could you say to Beth regarding her impending divorce?

_____

_____

_____

Day 3

1. Read 1 Peter 4: 12-13.

   a. How does Peter tell you not to think when problems come upon you?

   _____

   _____

   _____

   b. How does he tell us to react?

   _____

   _____

   _____

   c. In your own words, explain what it means to partake of Christ's suffering.

   _____

   _____

   _____

d. What is the result of partaking of Christ's suffering?

_____

_____

_____

2. Consider this statement "Christ did not die to make our earthly life comfortable; He died to make our eternity comfortable." Do you agree? Why or why not??

_____

_____

_____

3. Why do problems such as breakup of relationships, diseases, sickness, death, etc. happen?

_____

_____

_____

Day 4

1. Explain the meaning of Matthew 5:45 in your own words.

_____

_____

_____

2. Examine your expectations about problems.

_____

_____

_____

   a. What were your expectations regarding problems before you
      became a Christian?

_____

_____

_____

   b. Have your expectations changed the longer you have been a
      Christian? Why or why not?

_____

_____

_____

3. Read 1 Peter 4:1. What message is Peter communicating?

_____

_____

_____

4. William Vander Haven said, "Joy is not the absence of trouble, but the presence of Christ." Do you agree? Why or why not?

_____

_____

_____

Day 5

1. Read 2 Timothy 2:3 and Fill in the blank.

You must therefore endure _____
as a good soldier of Christ Jesus Christ.

2. Read Acts 14:22. How does this verse impact your expectations regarding problems?

_____

_____

_____

3. Read James 1:2-4

   a. Why do you think the writer says "When you fall into various problems" instead of "If you fall into various problems"?

_____

_____

_____

b. What should our attitude be when we face problems?

_____

_____

_____

c. Why should we have that attitude?

_____

_____

_____

d. Do you have that attitude? Why or why not?

_____

_____

_____

4. Can you think of a time in your life when a problem helped you become more patient? Describe the circumstances.

_____

_____

_____

5. C.S. Lewis said: "I didn't go to religion to make me happy. I always knew a bottle of Port would do that. If you want a religion to make you feel really comfortable, I certainly don't recommend Christianity." Do you agree? Why or why not?

_____

_____

_____

Day 6

1. Read Philippians 4:11. How did Paul describe his state of mind? Have you ever had this state of mind during problems? Why or why not?

_____

_____

_____

2. Why do you think Paul could have that state of mind despite being in prison awaiting execution?

_____

_____

_____

3. In view of Paul's state of mind, do you think he expected to have problems? Explain your answer.

_____

_____

_____

Day 7

Read Romans 8:28.

1. Do you think "all things" include problems? Why or why not?

_____

_____

_____

2. Are there truths in this verse that contradict the ideas we hear in the world? If so, what are they?

_____

_____

_____

3. Are there truths in this verse that contradict your ideas? If so, what are they?

_____

_____

_____

4. In view of this verse, what changes do you think God would want you to make in your attitude toward problems?

_____

_____

_____

5. Imagine that a friend, neighbor or co-worker is considering becoming a Christian asks what he/she should expect regarding problems. What would you tell him/her?

_____

_____

_____

Week

2

Distinguish Between Happiness and Joy

Focal Verse

Rejoice always. (1 Thessalonians 5:16)

N otice that Paul did not say, "Be happy always." People often confuse happiness with joy. I believe there are distinct differences. I will use three of Paula's roles to illustrate that point.

Paula, the wife

Paula has been married to Ben for twenty-two years. As with many married folks, people often ask Paula, "Are you happily married?" Like most people, Paula considers what is happening at the moment. She recognizes that "happiness" depends on "happenings", or the circumstances at a particular time. If things are going well and there are no pressing issues, she is likely to say she is happily married. But, if things are not going well, she is likely to say she is not happily married.

On the other hand, Paula recognizes that joy is not related to "happenings" or circumstances, but grows out of the state of her heart, her overall view of her relationship with Ben and her relationship with God. Therefore, she would say that she is joyfully married, even if there are issues about which she is not happy.

Paula, the manager

Paula is a nurse manager for a large metropolitan hospital. She is responsible for the quality of patient care in an acute care unit. She oversees all personnel and budget matters and she must create an environment that engages and inspires nurses and patient care technicians to deliver the highest quality of patient care.

Like many working people, Paula faces difficult situations. She deals with sick people, employee/employee and employee/patient conflict and sometimes she struggles to meet the desired patient care outcomes. Because of "happenings" Paula is not always happy. However, she is always joyful because she believes God has called her to this work and she sees how He is using her to make a difference in peoples' lives.

Paula, the mom

Paula and Ben have three children, ages 15, 17 and 19. Because of some of the "happenings" (attitudes toward schoolwork, rebellion against authority, choice of friends, etc.), Paula is not always a happy mom. However, she considers her children precious gifts from God and she absolutely loves and adores each one. Therefore, she is always a joyful mom.

In the final analysis, whether in her role as a wife, manager or mom, Paula understands that happiness is based on having situations, people, or events align with her expectations. Joy, on the other hand, is contentment based on the assurance that God is in control of every situation and that He works every situation for good.

Despite being in chains in a Roman prison, this distinction enabled the Apostle Paul to say Rejoice in the Lord always. Again I will say, rejoice. (Philippians 4:4)

Questions for discussion, reflection and application

1. Do you agree with Paula's distinction between happiness and joy as it pertains to her role as a wife, manager and mom? Why or why not?

_____

_____

_____

2. How would you describe the difference between happiness and joy to a friend?

_____

_____

_____

3. Think of Christians that you know. Would you say they experience more happiness or joy?

_____

_____

_____

4. Which do you experience more frequently – happiness or joy?
   Why?

_____

_____

_____

Day 2

1. Happiness is based on "happenings", so if things are going the
   way you like, you are happy. If things are not going the way you
   like, you are not happy. Do you agree? Why or why not?

_____

_____

_____

2. Happiness is temporary or fleeting; joy is permanent. Do you
   agree? Why or why not?

_____

_____

_____

3. Based on Luke 2:10-11. What is the source for joy?

_____

_____

_____

4. Read John 15:11. What does it mean to have your joy full?

_____

_____

_____

Day 3

1. Explain what it means to rejoice always.

_____

_____

_____

2. Is it possible to rejoice always? Why or why not?

_____

_____

_____

3. Read 2 Corinthians 6:10.

   a. Does rejoicing mean never experiencing sorrow? Why or why not?

_____

_____

_____

b. Describe a circumstance in which you were sorrowful, yet rejoiced?

_____

_____

_____

3. Read: Philippians 1:12-14. Give three reasons why Paul rejoiced during his imprisonment:

a. _____

b. _____

c. _____

Day 4

1. Based on John 16:22 can anyone or any "happening" take away your joy? Do you have trouble accepting that? Why or why not?

_____

_____

_____

2. Read Philippians 4:4 - What does it mean to rejoice in the Lord?

_____

_____

_____

3. What encouragement does Paul offer in Philippians 4:13 and 4:19 to help you rejoice?

_____

_____

_____

Day 5

1. Can your level of joy cause you to experience more happiness? Why or why not?

_____

_____

_____

2. Based on Matthew 21:12-13, would you say Jesus was always happy? Why or why not?

_____

_____

_____

3. Read Hebrews 12:2, would you say Jesus was always joyful, even during problems?

_____

_____

_____

4. Read 1 Thessalonians 5:16 – 18 and complete the following sentences: _____ always. _____ continually. For this is the _____ of God in Christ Jesus for you.

5. Explain the phrase "For this is the will of God in Christ for you."

_____

_____

_____

Day 6

1. Read James 1:2. Why do you think James did not say "Count it all happiness when you fall into various trials?"

_____

_____

_____

2. Read Psalm 16:11 and fill in the blank. In your presence is fullness of _____.

3. Fill in the blank in Matthew 25:23. Enter into the _____ _____ of the Lord. What, if any, significance do you place on the choice of words?

Day 7

1. Can you think of a person who is joyful, even in the midst of problems? What do you think makes the person joyful?

_____

_____

_____

2. If you focus on God instead of your circumstances, you will have joy, even if you are not happy. Do you agree? Why or why not?

_____

_____

_____

3. Joy is not found in riches or well-being, in human fame or power, or any human achievement, but in God alone. Do you agree? Why or why not?

_____

_____

_____

Week

Acknowledge that you Direct your Emotions

Focal Verse

For as he thinks in his heart, so is he. (Proverbs 23:7)

"I am beyond angry because my boss assigned me a new, short-deadline project without relieving me of any of my existing projects", Jonathan muttered to his wife, Carol.

Jonathan's blaming his boss for his emotions is commonplace. This is based on a common myth that people, events and circumstances dictate how we feel. So, when people, events and circumstances do not align with our expectations, we blame them for our feelings.

In reality, our thoughts about people, events or circumstances determine our feelings, not the people, events or circumstances themselves. Proverbs 23:7 says: As he thinks in his heart, so is he.

While Jonathan has zero control over his boss assigning him projects, he has one hundred percent control over his thoughts and feelings about the assignment of projects.

Let me give you a simple illustration of how your thoughts determine your feelings:

Imagine that a friend has agreed to meet you and does not show up at the agreed-upon time.

You think...	You probably feel...
My friend was in an accident.	Worried, concerned.
My friend lied. She never intended to meet me.	Angry, disappointed, hurt.
I get to go home and finish a project.	Relieved, happy.

Notice that the same event – your friend not showing up at the agreed-upon time – produced three different feelings depending on what you thought.

But the process does not stop there. The way you think determines how you feel, your feelings determine your actions, and your actions usually determine your outcomes.

Let's look at a Biblical example of this playing out.

Situation: All of the other Israelites were dreadfully afraid of Goliath. (1 Samuel 17:24)

David's thought: Since God had delivered him from the paw of a lion and the paw of a bear, David thought God would give him victory over Goliath. (1 Samuel 17:37)

David's feeling: He felt confident.

David's action:

» He volunteered to fight Goliath. (1 Samuel 17:32)

» Speaking to Goliath, David said: "You come to me with a sword, javelin, and spear, but I come to you in the name of the Lord of hosts, the God of the armies of Israel, whom you have defiled. (1 Samuel 17:45)

» He struck Goliath in the forehead with a stone from his sling-shot. (1 Samuel 17:49)

Outcome: Goliath was killed instantly. (1 Samuel 17:50)

So, if you want to change the way you feel, it always starts in your mind. That is why the Apostle Paul tells us "Do not be conformed to this world, but be transformed by the renewing of your mind." (Romans 12:2)

Questions for discussion, reflection and application

1. Read Philippians 4:13. Do you have the power to control what you think? Why or why not?

_____

_____

_____

2. Read John 16:22. Can anyone steal your joy? Do you have trouble accepting that? Why or why not?

_____

_____

_____

3. Read 1 John 4:4. - Can Satan rob you of your joy? Do you have trouble accepting that? Why or why not?

_____

_____

_____

4. Can any circumstance rob you of your joy? Why or why not?

_____

_____

_____

5. Read Genesis 4:1 - 8.

   a. What were God's instructions to Cain? (v.6 – 7)

_____

_____

_____

   b. Do you believe Cain had the ability to control his thoughts and emotions? Why or why not?

_____

_____

_____

Day 2

1. Read Romans 12:1–2.

   a. What does Paul warn us against?

_____

_____

_____

b. What does he say must happen in order to transform our lives?

_____

_____

_____

c. What does it mean to "Renew your mind?"

_____

_____

_____

2. Based on 2 Corinthians 10:5

a. How can you renew our mind?

_____

_____

_____

b. What does it look like to take each thought captive?

_____

_____

_____

Note: You will get to practice this process during Week 5 – Challenge and Replace Joy-Robbing Thoughts.

3. Read Isaiah 26:3.

    a. What is the impact of keeping your mind on God?

_____

_____

_____

    b. Why is this possible?

_____

_____

_____

4. Read 2 Timothy 1:7 – What does it mean to have a sound mind?

_____

_____

_____

5. Read Proverbs 17:22. How does joy impact your health?

_____

_____

_____

Day 3

1. Describe a current circumstance in which you are blaming someone or some circumstance for your lack of joy.

_____

_____

_____

2. How do you feel when you blame someone or some circumstance for your lack of joy? Circle all that apply. (Examples: Angry, frustrated, helpless, overwhelmed, inadequate, disappointed, upset, tense, disgusted, hopeless, hurt, annoyed, anxious, resentful, rejected, uncertain, perplexed, diminished, dissatisfied, vulnerable, woeful, empty, uneasy, distressed

_____

_____

_____

3. How do you act when you blame someone or some circumstance for your lack of joy? Circle all that apply. (Examples: argue, yell, cry, feel sorry for yourself, smoke, drink, abuse substances, withdraw, worry, overeat, lose your appetite, lose sleep, procrastinate, shop, gossip, attack others, call out sick, have accidents, lose things, use poor problem-solving skills, experience poor concentration, develop forgetfulness, become confused, become unable to make decisions). Feel free to add to the list.

_____

_____

_____

4. Acknowledge that it is your fault that you feel the way you feel.

_____

_____

_____

5. How do you feel now that you have taken responsibility for your feelings?

   I have listed a few words. Circle those that apply. Feel free to add words.

   Encouraged, rejuvenated, relieved, energetic, calm, content, free and easy, hopeful, peaceful, at ease, relaxed, confident, satisfied, great, joyful, delighted, optimistic, comfortable, reassured, great, delighted, thankful, confident, loving, enlightened, supported, liberated, empowered

6. How do you act now that you have taken responsibility for your feelings?

_____

_____

_____

Day 4

1. Read Proverbs 4:23.

   a. Why should we guard our hearts?

   _____

   _____

   _____

   b. Does the verse reinforce or contradict Proverbs 23:7? Why or why not?

   _____

   _____

   _____

2. Your thoughts can limit who you are, what you do and what you become. Do you agree? Why or why not?

   _____

   _____

   _____

3. Read Lamentations 3:1-25.

    a. Compare Jeremiah's emotions in verses 1 through 20 with his emotions in verses 22 through 25.

_____

_____

_____

    b. Did his circumstances change or remain the same?

_____

_____

_____

    c. What happened in verse 21 to change his emotions?

_____

_____

_____

    d. Can you apply this the next time you are facing a problem?

_____

_____

_____

4. Read Proverbs 23:7. If you have negative thoughts, you will become a negative person? Do you agree? Why or why not?

_____

_____

_____

Day 5

1. Read John 14:27. When facing a problem:

a. What are the benefits of focusing your thoughts on Jesus?

_____

_____

_____

b. Can focusing your thoughts on the world bring you peace?

_____

_____

_____

2. Read Philippians 4:8-9. What is the result of meditating on
things that are true, noble, just, pure, lovely, of good report and
the things you learned, received, heard and saw in Paul?

_____

_____

_____

3. Read Ephesians 4:26.

   a. How does Paul tell us to handle our anger?

_____

_____

_____

   b. Why do you think he tells us to handle our anger this way?

_____

_____

_____

4. Read Romans 8:1. How does this verse apply if guilt is robbing you of joy?

_____

_____

_____

Day 6

1. Chuck Swindoll said: "Life is 10% what happens to you and 90% how you respond to it." Do you agree? Why or why not?

_____

_____

_____

2. Read Deuteronomy 34:8.

   a. How long did God allow the people to mourn when Moses died?

_____

_____

_____

   b. What (if any) implications might that have for us today?

_____

_____

_____

3. How does Revelation 21:4 affect your joy?

_____

_____

_____

4. How much do your emotions affect your actions on a typical day?

_____

_____

_____

Day 7

1. Which unwanted emotion do you experience most frequently?

_____

_____

_____

2. What advice would you give to a friend who is struggling with anger, stress, worry or fear?

_____

_____

_____

3. Many Christians complain about being stressed out. Read Philippians 4:8. Does it show you how to reduce stress? Why or why not?

_____

_____

_____

4. Fill in the blank in Colossians 3:15. And let the _____ _____ of God rule in your hearts, to which also you were called in one body; and be thankful.

Week

4

Decide to Rejoice

Focal Verse:

Even though the fig trees are all destroyed, and there is neither blossom left nor fruit; though the olive crops all fail, and the fields lie barren; even if the flocks die in the fields and the cattle barns are empty, yet I will rejoice in the Lord; I will be happy in the God of my salvation. (Habakkuk 3:17-18 TLB)

In the beginning of the book of Habakkuk, Habakkuk begs God to explain why God's chosen people are allowed to suffer in their captivity and why God will not save them. (Habakkuk 1:1-4). The Lord basically tells him, "You wouldn't believe it if I told you" (Habakkuk 1: 5-11). At this point Habakkuk says, "Ok, you are God, but still tell me more about why this is happening" (Habakkuk 1:17-2:1). God gives him more information, and then tells the earth to be silent before Him (Habakkuk 2:2-20). With this in mind, Habakkuk writes a prayer expressing his strong faith in God, indicating that he has decided to rejoice in the Lord, despite his problems.

He expresses part of that prayer in Chapter 3:17-18, in which he said, "Even though the fig trees are all destroyed, and there is neither blossom left nor fruit; though the olive crops all fail, and the fields lie barren; even if the flocks die in the fields and the cattle barns are empty, yet I will rejoice in the Lord; I will be happy in the God of my salvation."

I want to highlight "Yet I will rejoice in the Lord." When we commit our life to Jesus Christ, His Holy Spirit takes up residence in our heart. With the Holy Spirit comes the free gift of joy. (Galatians 5:22) However, God does not force us to use the free gift. We are free to choose whether or not to use it. It is like getting a pre-approved credit card. Even though you have the card, you are free to choose whether or not to use it. Choosing to use it requires activating the card by either going online or calling a toll free number. Likewise, choosing to accept the free gift of joy requires making a conscious decision.

Although deciding to rejoice while in the midst of trouble is not the natural human response, Habakkuk made that decision.

Questions for discussion, reflection, and application

Philippians 4:4 commands us to Rejoice in the Lord always: and again I say, Rejoice. It was so important that Paul repeated it.

1. When you face problems are you more likely to obey the command or follow your feelings. Why?

_____

_____

_____

2. Praising God, giving thanks and serving others are examples of rejoicing when facing problems. Do you agree? Why or why not?

_____

_____

_____

3. Shock, anger, sadness, fear are examples of following your feelings when facing problems. Do you agree? Why or why not?

_____

_____

_____

4. How do most Christians that you know decide to respond when facing problems?

_____

_____

_____

5. How do you decide to respond when facing problems?

_____

_____

_____

6. Is it possible to rejoice always? Why or why not?

_____

_____

_____

Day 2

1. Did God give Adam and Eve the freedom to decide whether or not to obey His command not to eat the forbidden fruit?

_____

_____

_____

2. Were there consequences of their decision? What were the consequences?

_____

_____

_____

3. Are there consequences to our decision to follow our feelings instead of following the command to rejoice? What are the consequences?

_____

_____

_____

4. Read Matthew 5:12.

a. What is the command?

_____

_____

_____

b. What is the consequence of obeying the command?

_____

_____

_____

5. Read 1 Peter 4:13.

   a. What is the command?

   _____

   _____

   _____

   b. What is the consequence of obeying the command?

   _____

   _____

   _____

6. Zig Ziglar said: "You are free to choose, but the choices you make today will determine what you will be, do and have in the tomorrows of your life." Do you agree? Why or why not?

   _____

   _____

   _____

7. You can decide to walk by sight (focus on circumstances) or walk by faith (focus on the fact that God is working behind the scenes). Do you agree? Why or why not?

   _____

   _____

   _____

Day 3

1. Read Philippians 4:6 .

   a. What did Paul identify as a major joy-robber?

   _____

   _____

   _____

   b. What did Paul say you can do to negate this joy-robber?

   _____

   _____

   _____

2. What other things prevent you from following the command to rejoice always?

   a. Things you think about yourself. Example: I will never succeed.

1. _____

2. _____

   b. Your expectations of others. Example: Having rules that others must follow.

1. _____

2. _____

c. Things over which you have no control. Example: the weather.

1. _____

2. _____

d. Things you do to yourself. Example: Taking responsibility for others' emotional well-being.

1. _____

2. _____

e. Things you do to others. Example: Judging others.

1. _____

2. _____

f. Things others do to you. Example: Exclude you from social gatherings.

1. _____

2. _____

g. Things others do not do to you. Example: Show empathy.

1. _____

2. _____

Feel free to add categories and issues.

Day 4

1. Read Philippians 4:8. Select 3 principles and explain how "thinking on these things" can help you rejoice in the midst of your problem.

_____

_____

_____

2. Read the following verses and identify why you should rejoice in problems:

a. James 1:2-3

_____

_____

_____

b. Romans 5:3-4

_____

_____

_____

3. List 3 things for which you are grateful right now.

a. _____

b. _____

c. _____

Day 5

1. Proverbs 4:23 (NLT) says: Guard your heart above all else, for it determines the course of your life (NLT).

   a. What does it mean to "guard your heart"?

   _____

   _____

   _____

   b. b. How can guarding your heart impact your choice of TV shows, books, radio stations and people with whom you associate?

   _____

   _____

   _____

2. Read Hebrews 10:25.

   a. a. How does the writer suggest you avail yourself of the resources of other believers?

   _____

   _____

   _____

b. Specifically, what can friends do to help you deal with a difficult circumstance?

_____

_____

_____

3. Read Job 13:15. Would you consider Job an example of someone who decided to rejoice despite his circumstances? Why or Why not?

_____

_____

_____

4. Read Isaiah 14:24. God is in control of everything, including problems that come into your life. Do you agree? Why or why not?

_____

_____

_____

Day 6

1. Does being joyful mean going around with a perpetual smile on your face? Why or why not?

_____

_____

_____

2. Read 2 Corinthians 6:10. Does being joyful mean never having pain or sorrow? Why or why not?

_____

_____

_____

3. Think about a time when you were faced with an unpleasant situation that was out of your control, yet you rejoiced. How were you able to do so?

_____

_____

_____

4. What would you say to a Christian friend who seeks your advice on how to deal with a problem?

_____

_____

_____

Day 7

1. Read 1 Peter 1:6

a. What promise does the verse give us about the duration of our problems?

_____

_____

_____

b. How does that promise impact your attitude towards problems?

_____

_____

_____

2. Read Romans 8:28-29. Name two reasons you can decide to rejoice during problems.

_____

_____

_____

3. Read Psalm 23:4. Would you say David had decided to rejoice, despite his circumstances? Why or why not?

_____

_____

_____

4. What difference would it make in the following areas of your life if you decided to follow the command to rejoice?

a. Your family

_____

_____

_____

b. Your work

_____

_____

_____

c. Your health

_____

_____

_____

d. Your relationships

_____

_____

_____

5. Read James 1:8. When it comes to deciding – what does James caution against? Why?

_____

_____

_____

6. What encouragement do you get from Psalm 118:24?

_____

_____

_____

Week

5

Challenge and Replace Joy-Robbing Thoughts

Focal Verse

We destroy arguments and every lofty opinion raised against the knowledge of God, and take every thought captive to obey Christ. (2 Corinthians 10:5 ESV)

As we discussed in week 3, thoughts lead to feelings. Therefore, joy-robbing thoughts lead to a lack of joy. So, in order to rejoice, you must challenge every thought you have. If the thought matches Jesus' word, continue thinking it. If the thought does not match Jesus' word, replace it with one that does.

Psalms 42 and 43 illustrates this process:

Illustration One

Joy-robbing thought: "My tears have been my food day and night." (Psalm 42:3)

Challenging the thought: "Why are you cast down, O my soul?" (Psalm 42:5)

Replacing the thought: "Hope in God." (Psalm 42:5)

Illustration Two

Joy-robbing thought: "Why have you forgotten me? As with the breaking of my bones. My enemies revile me." (Psalm 42:9 - 10)

Challenging the thought: "Why are you cast down, O my soul?" (Psalm 42:11a)

Replacing the thought: "Hope in God." (Psalm 42:11b)

Illustration Three

Joy-robbing thought: "Why do you cast me off?" (Psalm 43:2)

Challenging the thought: "Why are you cast down, O my soul?" (Psalm 43: 5)

Replacing the thought: "Hope in God." (Psalm 43:5)

The Result of challenging and replacing thoughts: Even though circumstances did not change, the Psalmists changed his perspective and said, "For I shall yet praise him." (Psalm 43:5)

Questions for discussion, reflection and application

1. Read Proverbs 23:7. Why is what you think so important?

_____

_____

_____

2. Jonathan Edwards said: "The ideas and images in men's minds are the invisible powers that constantly govern them." Do you agree? Why or why not?

_____

_____

_____

3. Read 2 Corinthians 10:4, 5.

   a. What influences your thoughts?

_____

_____

_____

   b. By tapping into the power of God's word, you can "manage your thoughts", i.e. take unwanted thoughts captive, rather than allowing unwanted thoughts to take you captive. Do you agree? Why or why not?

_____

_____

_____

4. Open the Contents section of *The Power to Rejoice: 21Days to Victory Over Your Problems.*

   a. Identify an area of your life in which you are experiencing problems, i.e. Work/Career, Physical Health, Emotional Health, Death, Financial, Family.

_____

_____

_____

   b. Proceed to the appropriate chapter.

_____

_____

_____

   c. Proceed to Step 3.

_____

_____

_____

d. Identify your thought about the problem. Example: I am about to have surgery and I am scared.

_____

_____

_____

e. Challenge the thought? Does it match God's word?

_____

_____

_____

f. If not, replace the thought with a verse from God's word from Day 1 through Day 21.

_____

_____

_____

g. Follow steps 4 through 9.

_____

_____

_____

Week

6

Act Based on what you know

Focal Verse

Be doers of the word and not hearers only,
deceiving yourselves. (James 1:22 MEV)

Imagine that you are with a close friend and he/she says "I really appreciate you as a friend, I am glad we get to spend time together," … and then pauses and adds …BUT….

If you are like me, "But" cancels the first part of the sentence and you focus on the second part because you recognize that this is what your friend really thinks or feels.

"I know the Bible says I should not worry", BUT….

This is an example of what I hear from Christians repeatedly. I wait for the second part of sentence, which is usually an explanation of the circumstances that is causing them to worry, e.g. "I have not found a job yet", "the x-ray showed a spot on my lung", "I may be headed for a divorce", etc.

This scenario represents a conflict between what we know and what we believe, or as James would say, being "double-minded." (James 1:8)

If we only know something, it is just one more fact we can recite from memory, e.g. there are 12 inches in a foot. On the other hand, if we both know and believe something, it implies confidence and trust and it changes how we view life's circumstances. The combination of knowing, believing and having faith in also influences our feelings, actions and often, the results.

The process works like this: We know something, then we believe it, and then have faith in what we believe and finally we take action.

The Gospel of Mark provides a great example of knowing, believing, feeling and acting in the story about the woman who was hemorrhaging. For twelve years she had experienced the indescribable discomfort and embarrassment of a blood flow that no physician could heal. To add to her misery, her extensive medical bills had caused her to become financially destitute. Mark summarizes the woman's despair this way: "She had suffered a great deal under the care of many doctors and had spent all she had, yet instead of getting better she grew worse" (Mark 5:26).

What the woman knew: She had heard about Jesus' healing power. (Mark 5:27)

What she believed and had faith in: Jesus could restore her health. She said, "If only I may touch his clothes, I shall be made well." (Mark 5:28).

How she felt: Confident based on what she knew, believed and had faith in.

Her actions: She pushed her way through the crowd and touched Jesus' garment. (Mark 5:27)

The Result: The minute she touched His garment she was healed. (Mark 5:29)

Jesus said to her, "Daughter, your faith has made you well. Go in peace and be healed of your affliction. (Mark 5:34)

Questions for reflection, discussion and application

Day 1

1. Belief and faith are not one and the same. Do you agree? Why or why not?

_____

_____

_____

2. Identify a circumstance in your life which is not going the way you would like.

    a. Do you believe God is in control of the circumstance? Why or why not?

    _____

    _____

    _____

    b. Do you have faith that God will use the circumstance for your good? Why or why not?

    _____

    _____

    _____

3. You cannot experience joy until you not only believe in God, but have unwavering faith in Him. Do you agree? Why or why not?

_____

_____

_____

4. Read Ecclesiastes 7:14 and answer the following questions:

   a. How are you responding to a current adverse circumstance?

_____

_____

_____

   b. How should you respond to it?

_____

_____

_____

   c. Does your response demonstrate faith?

_____

_____

_____

   d. What are you learning from the adversity?

_____

_____

_____

e. How can God use the adversity in your life?

_____

_____

_____

5. Fill in the blank from 2 Corinthians 5:7.

a. We walk by _____ and not by

_____ .

b. What does the verse mean to you?

_____

_____

_____

Day 2

1. 1. Read James 2:20 and fill in the blank. Faith without works is

_____ .

What does the verse mean to you?

_____

_____

_____

2. How do think you would react if you had a persistent health issue like the woman in Mark's story?

_____

_____

_____

3. If there were a woman like this where you live how would people respond to her?

_____

_____

_____

4. How would you respond to such a woman?

_____

_____

_____

5. Read Mark 5:34. What did Jesus mean by "Your faith has made you well?"

_____

_____

_____

Day 3

1. Isaiah 55:8-9 and fill in the blanks.

For my _____ are not your

_____, neither are your _____

_____ my _____ , says

the Lord. For as the heavens are _____ than

the earth, so are my ways _____ than your

ways and my thoughts than your thoughts.

2. God's purposes are beyond your understanding. Do you agree?
   Why or why not?

_____

_____

_____

3. Read Job 13:15. How close can you come to saying, as Job did,
   "Though he slay me, yet will I trust him?"

_____

_____

_____

4. What impact does Psalm 23:4 have on you when you are in the midst of a problem?

_____

_____

_____

5. Read Matthew 19:26 How does it affect your faith and actions?

_____

_____

_____

Day 4

1. Read Matthew 9:18-25.

   a. Did the ruler demonstrate belief, faith or both? Why do you say that? (v.18)

_____

_____

_____

   b. What did Jesus say to the crowd at the ruler's house? (v.24)

_____

_____

_____

c. What was the outcome of Jesus' visit to the ruler's house? (v.25)

_____

_____

_____

2. Read 1 Thessalonians 1:6. Would you consider this an example of acting based on what they knew? Why or why not?

_____

_____

_____

3. Imagine that a friend is going through a difficult problem and angrily asks, "How can you have faith in a God who allows this to happen?" How would you respond?

_____

_____

_____

4. Explain James 1:22 in your own words.

_____

_____

_____

5. What does it mean when the writer of Hebrews said in verse 11:10 that "Faith is the assurance of things hoped for, the conviction of things not seen."

_____

_____

_____

6. Do you find it hard to have faith during problems? Why or why not?

_____

_____

_____

Day 5

1. Read James 2:15, 16. What example does James give of empty words that do not demonstrate faith?

_____

_____

_____

2. We do not develop faith by doing good actions; good actions come as the result of faith. Do you agree? Why or why not?

_____

_____

_____

3. Read the story of Paul's and Silas' imprisonment in Acts 16:22-35.

   a. What reaction did Paul and Silas have? (v.25)

_____

_____

_____

   b. What was the result of their actions? (v.27 – 35)

_____

_____

_____

   c. Did Paul and Silas act based on what they knew? Why or why not?

_____

_____

_____

   d. Would God not be touched by your praises today, despite your circumstance?

_____

_____

_____

e. Would He not do the same thing for you today that He did for Paul and Silas? (v.35)

_____

_____

_____

4. Read Matthew 5:11. How does it compare to Paul's and Silas' imprisonment?

_____

_____

_____

5. Give an example of when you acted based on what you knew, even when it made no sense.

a. What was the situation?

_____

_____

_____

b. What did you do?

_____

_____

_____

c. What was the outcome?

_____

_____

_____

Day 6

1. Read Numbers 13:1-33, 14:1-30.

   a. What report did ten of the spies give to Moses and Aaron? (Chapter 13:32 - 33)

   _____

   _____

   _____

   b. What report did Joshua and Caleb give? (Chapter 14: 6-9)

   _____

   _____

   _____

   c. Who acted based on what they knew, Caleb and Joshua or the other ten spies?

   _____

   _____

   _____

d. What was the result? (Chapter 14:30)

_____

_____

_____

e. Why did God bring about that result?

_____

_____

_____

2. A.W. Tozer said: "Any faith that must be supported by evidence of the senses is not faith at all." Do you agree? Why or why not?

_____

_____

_____

3. Dr. Tony Evans said: "Faith is acting like it is so, even if it is not so, so that it might be so, simply because God said so." Do you agree? Why or why not?

_____

_____

_____

4. Jackie knows that "to die is to gain." However, when her husband, Joseph, died she was angry with God. She stopped going to church, reading her Bible and praying. Was Jackie's reaction an example of acting based on what she knew? Why or why not?

_____

_____

_____

Day 7

1. Read Daniel 3: 1-30.

   a. What was Shadrach's, Meshach's and Abed-Nego's response to King Nebuchadnezzar's decree to worship his image? (v.16-18)

   _____

   _____

   _____

   b. Was their response an example of acting based on what they knew? Why or why not?

   _____

   _____

   _____

c. What happened once they were in the furnace? (v.24-26)

_____

_____

_____

d. What was the King's response to what he had witnessed? (v.29)

_____

_____

_____

2. Read Genesis 22:1-18. How did Abraham's actions support his faith?

_____

_____

_____

3. Based on James 2:21 - 22, how was Abraham's faith made complete by his actions?

_____

_____

_____

4. Read Joshua 2:1-24 and 6:20-25.

_____

_____

_____

a. How did Rehab demonstrate her faith? (v.1-24)

_____

_____

_____

b. What was the result of her actions? (v.6:20-25)

_____

_____

_____

Week

7

Focus on the Benefits of Problems

Focal Verse

And we know that in all things God works for the good of those who love him, who have been called according to his purpose. (Romans 8:28 NIV)

Engineers tell us that in order for metal to be used safely it must be pure. The purification process involves repeated testing by having the metal go through extreme heat. It must then be melted and molded to fit the designer's purpose.

We are like metal; before God can use us for his purpose, we must be purified by being tested by extreme heat (problems) and molded. That is what happened to Joseph.

Imagine that you are seventeen years old and:

» The people to whom you are closest, your siblings, throw you into a pit; rescue you from the pit, only to sell you to a slave trader.

» Your boss, whom you have dutifully served with impeccable loyalty and integrity, is quick to believe a lie about you and subsequently throws you into prison.

» An associate, whom you had helped solve a personal dilemma, breaks a promise, resulting in your spending several years in jail.

These were precisely the things that happened to Joseph. (Genesis 37 – 50)

a. Joseph's brothers cast him into a pit. (Genesis 37:24) Later, they rescued him from the pit, only to sell him into slavery. (Genesis 37:28)

b. Joseph got promoted from slave to supervisor. However, after resisting Potiphar's wife's sexual advances, she falsely accused him of attempting to rape her. Potiphar placed Joseph in prison. (Genesis 39: 20)

c. While Joseph was in prison, Pharaoh became angry with his chief butler and chief baker and had them imprisoned and placed into Joseph's custody. (Genesis 40:1 – 4) Both had dreams which Joseph interpreted. (Genesis 40:5 - 8) He interpreted the Chief Butler's dream to mean he would be returned to his former position. (Genesis 40:13). Joseph interpreted the Chief Baker's dream to mean that he would be hanged. (Genesis 40:19)

» Joseph asked the Chief Butler to put in a good word for him with the Pharaoh and get him out of prison. (Genesis 40:14) Just as Joseph had predicted, the chief baker was hanged and the chief butler was promoted. However, the chief butler did not keep his promise to Joseph to mention Joseph to Pharaoh. (Genesis 40:23) So, Joseph remained in prison for two more years.

Although Joseph was in slavery or prison for thirteen years, he ultimately was released and carried out God's purpose. (Genesis 50:20)

When bad things happen to "good" people, we tend to ask "Why". A more appropriate question is "How", as in "How is God working this situation for good?" Joseph's story is a compelling example of that question being answered.

Questions for discussion, reflection, and application

Read Romans 8:28 and answer the following multiple-choice questions:

1. To whom is this verse addressed?

   a. Only people whose lives are full of good things

   b. Only the Roman Saints.

   c. Everyone who loves God and is called according to His purpose, including Joseph

2. Based on your response to the question above, do you qualify for this promise?

   a. Yes

   b. No

   c. I'm not sure

Why?

_____

_____

_____

3. How many things (or circumstances) are included in God's purpose?

   a. Some things

   b. Only the "good" things

   c. Only the "bad" things

   d. "Good" and "bad" things

4. When it comes to "good", your definition is:

   a. The same as God's

   b. Similar to God's

   c. Not even close to God's

5. What are these "things," that are mentioned in Romans 8:28? (Circle as many as apply.)

   a. Health

   b. Finances

   c. Relationships

   d. Career

   e. Freedom and/or incarceration

6. How do all of these "things" work for good?

   a. Roll of the dice – sometimes you win, sometimes you lose

   b. Fate

   c. Luck

   d. God works them

7. Based on your response to the question above, when is God in control?

   a. At the beginning of all things

   b. At the end of all things

   c. At every point in between

   d. All of the above

   e. Never

1. According to Genesis 50:20 what was God's purpose in Joseph's story?

_____

_____

_____

2. Read Genesis 37:5 – 8. What did God reveal to Joseph through a dream about his future position?

_____

_____

_____

3. What is the common statement in verses Genesis 39:2 - 3, Genesis 39:21 and Genesis 39:23?

a. What does the statement mean?

_____

_____

_____

b. How does the statement support or contradict Matthew 28:20 and Hebrews 13:5?

_____

_____

_____

c. What encouragement can you draw from the statement when you are going through problems?

_____

_____

_____

4. Based on Genesis 39:3, do you believe God used Joseph to witness to Potiphar?

a. Why or why not?

_____

_____

_____

b. Do you believe God can use you to witness to others as you are going through problems?

_____

_____

_____

c. If so, what type of attitude must you maintain in order to be effective?

_____

_____

_____

5. As a slave Joseph served Potiphar. (Genesis 39:4) While in prison, he served the other prisoners by interpreting their dreams. (Genesis 40:1 – 13) When you face problems, do you serve others? Why or why not?

_____

_____

_____

6. Based on Genesis 41:39 – 41, what was Joseph's ultimate appointment?

_____

_____

_____

7. Do you think Joseph's experience as a slave and prisoner:

   a. Made him more qualified to serve as Prime Minister

   b. Less qualified to serve

   c. Had no impact on his ability to serve

Why?

_____

_____

_____

8. Read Psalm 105: 17 – 19. Describe a time when you believed God was testing your character.

_____

_____

_____

Day 3

1. Read 2 Corinthians 1:3-4

   a. How do you benefit from problems? (v.4)

_____

_____

_____

b. Describe how you or someone you know received this benefit.

_____

_____

_____

2. Read James 1:3

a. How do you benefit from problems?

_____

_____

_____

b. Describe how you or someone you know received this benefit.

_____

_____

_____

3. Read Romans 5:3.

a. How do you benefit from problems?

_____

_____

_____

b. Describe how you or someone you know received his benefit.

_____

_____

_____

4. Read 1 Peter 1:6-7.

   a. How do you benefit from problems?

_____

_____

_____

   b. Did Joseph receive this benefit?

_____

_____

_____

   c. Have you received this benefit?

_____

_____

_____

5. Read 2 Corinthians 1:9.

   a. How do you benefit from problems?

_____

_____

_____

b. Describe how you or someone you know received this benefit.

_____

_____

_____

6. John Piper said: "We will have everything we need in this life, including painful things necessary to bring us to glory." Do you agree? Why or why not?

_____

_____

_____

Day 4

1. Read Romans 8:29.

   a. How do you benefit from problems?

_____

_____

_____

   b. Describe how you or someone you know received this benefit.

_____

_____

_____

2. Problems are part of God's conforming process for our lives. Rather than complaining when problems come our way, we should rejoice as we consider the value they produce. Do you agree? Why or why not?

_____

_____

_____

3. Read Psalm 119:71

a. What was the Psalmist's attitude toward problems?

_____

_____

_____

b. What benefits did the Psalmist gain from his problems?

_____

_____

_____

4. Charles Spurgeon said: "They who dive in the sea of affliction bring up rare pearls." Do you agree? Why or why not?

_____

_____

_____

Day 5

1. 1. Read Matthew 5:11–12. Is there a reward given for suffering? If so, who receives the reward?

_____

_____

_____

2. Read Revelation 2:10.

   a. In what ways should the prospect of future reward and glory encourage you as you face problems?

_____

_____

_____

   b. How can you encourage others when they are suffering?

_____

_____

_____

3. We typically complain about how long we must endure a problem. Raymond Edman said: "Delay never thwarts God's purpose; it only polishes His instruments." What do you think that means? Do you agree? Why or why not?

_____

_____

_____

4. Identify an area of your life in which you are currently experiencing a problem, i.e. Work/Career Problems, Physical Health Problems, Emotional Health Problems, Death, Financial Problems, Family Problems.

Has the problem caused you to decide to move closer to God and His Word or caused you to decide to pull you away from God and His Word? Why?

_____

_____

_____

Day 6

1. Rick Warren said: "Your most effective ministry will come out of your deepest hurt." Do you agree? Why or why not?

_____

_____

_____

Describe how have you used a personal hurt to minister to others?

_____

_____

_____

2. Read John 15:2. What is the process of being of conformed to Jesus' image?

_____

_____

_____

3. Based on Job 42:2. Can anything stop God from achieving His purpose?

_____

_____

_____

4. Read 2 Timothy 2:12. Enduring problems enable us to _____ _____ with Jesus.

a. What does that mean?

_____

_____

_____

b. How does that impact your view of problems?

_____

_____

_____

Day 7

1. Faith is like a muscle. It can only be developed through repeated use. Problems cause us to develop our faith muscle. Do you agree? Why or why not?

_____

_____

_____

2. Read James 1:1-4

a. What is your usual response when you face problems?

_____

_____

_____

b. Based on verse 2, what should a Christian's attitude be when facing problems?

_____

_____

_____

c. How can you receive "Wisdom"? Share a time when you received wisdom.

_____

_____

_____

d. When seeking wisdom what must you guard against? (v.6)

_____

_____

_____

Week

8

Make Gratitude a Habit

Focal Verse

Whatever happens, keep thanking God because of Jesus Christ. This is what God wants you to do. (1 Thessalonians 5:18 CEV)

In 2008 a young Australian woman, Hailey Bartholomew, found that she wasn't enjoying life. She described herself as feeling lost and stuck on a treadmill. It was almost inexplicable. She was married to a man she loved and had beautiful children who held her heart. So why was she feeling so down about her life? Hailey sought the counsel of a nun, who advised her to spend time each day reflecting on something for which she was grateful. Hailey began a project called "365 grateful". Every day she took a photograph of something for which she was grateful.

It changed her life, for it allowed her to see things she had never noticed. Hailey had always thought of her husband as unromantic. One day she took a picture of him serving up dinner, the thing which she was grateful for that day. She noticed for the first time that the largest portion of pie was placed on her plate. She realized that the largest portion was always placed on her plate and that this was one small but profound way her husband showed his care for her. Hailey had found mothering a "boring job", but as she took photos of her children holding out their hands to her, playing and exploring, she discovered how much joy and wonder there was in her world.

Through the art of gratitude Hailey found herself lifted out of her rut and she began celebrating her life.

Questions for discussion, reflection and application

Day 1

1. Why do you think God has commanded us to be thankful? Do you feel comfortable with this command? Why or why not?

_____

_____

_____

2. Can being thankful give you joy? Why or why not?

_____

_____

_____

3. Is it possible to be thankful in the midst of a problem? Why or why not?

_____

_____

_____

4. Job had it all and lost it all. What was his response? (Job 1:20-22)

_____

_____

_____

5. What are some blessings for which you are thankful right now?

_____

_____

_____

Day 2

1. Read Luke 22:17 and Luke 22:19.

   a. What did Jesus do right before He went to the cross?

   _____

   _____

   _____

   b. How was Jesus able to do this when facing a horrible death?

   _____

   _____

   _____

c. How does Jesus' action impact you as you face problems?

_____

_____

_____

2. When you are thanking God, where is your focus – on God or your circumstances? How does your focus impact how you feel?

_____

_____

_____

3. Who do you know who is a model of expressing gratitude? Why do you consider him/her a model?

_____

_____

_____

4. Read Philippians 4:6-7.

a. Can expressing gratitude relieve anxiety?

_____

_____

_____

b. Have you ever experienced this?

_____

_____

_____

c. If so, describe the circumstances.

_____

_____

_____

5. Is it possible for your gratitude during problems to lead others to Christ? Why or why not?

_____

_____

_____

Day 3

1. Read 1 Thessalonians 5:16 – 18. Is it possible to rejoice always without giving thanks in everything? Why or why not?

_____

_____

_____

2. Read Daniel 6:10.

    a. What did Daniel do when he learned that some men were plotting to destroy him?

_____

_____

_____

    b. Is his response an example of obeying 1 Thessalonians 5:18? Why or why not?

_____

_____

_____

3. Read Ephesians 5:20.

    a. When should we give thanks?

_____

_____

_____

    b. For what should we give thanks?

_____

_____

_____

c. Does that include problems? Why or why not?

_____

_____

_____

4. What is the indescribable gift mentioned in 2 Corinthians 9:15 for which we should give thanks?

_____

_____

_____

5. What would you include in a "Thank You" letter to God?

_____

_____

_____

Day 4

1. Luke 17:11-19 tells a story of lepers being healed.

a. Why do you think only one of the ten expressed gratitude?

_____

_____

_____

b. Is ingratitude prevalent today?

_____

_____

_____

c. Are you ever guilty of ingratitude? Why or why not?

_____

_____

_____

d. Do you ever feel gratitude but never get around to expressing it? If so, why?

_____

_____

_____

2. According to Psalm 44:8, how frequently should we express thanksgiving?

_____

_____

_____

3. How can gratitude help you experience God while you are in the midst of a problem?

_____

_____

_____

4. The preposition in 1 Thessalonians 5:18 is worth noting. We are commanded to thank God "in" all circumstances, not "for" all circumstances. While we may never be grateful for certain painful experiences, we can still be grateful during them.

What are some things for which you are thankful even "in" difficult circumstances?

_____

_____

_____

5. Thanks and hope work together. We wait expectantly, with hope, believing that He will keep His promises to see us through the hard times and provide all we need. Do you agree? Why or why not?

_____

_____

_____

Day 5

1. One reason for not thanking God in all circumstances is that we do not trust Him to work everything for good. Do you agree? Why or why not?

_____

_____

_____

2. How can gratitude impact your relationship with God?

_____

_____

_____

3. Name one thing for which you thankful regarding your:

   a. Spouse

   b. Children

   c. Neighbors

   d. Co-workers

   e. Fellow believers

4. Charles Spurgeon said "When joy and prayer are married their first born child is gratitude." Do you agree? Why or why not?

_____

_____

_____

Day 6

1. In 2 Corinthians 12:7, Paul went from asking God to remove the thorn to thanking Him for it. Have you ever thanked the Lord for a thorn? Why or why not?

_____

_____

_____

2. Why should your gratitude extend beyond what you have in the bank, closet or driveway?

_____

_____

_____

3. Charles Spurgeon said: "An enlightened man is grateful to God for temporal blessings; but he is much more grateful to God for spiritual blessings, for temporal blessings do not last long; they are soon gone. Temporal blessings are not definite marks of divine favor, since God gives them to the unworthy, and to the wicked, as well as to the righteous." Do you agree? Why or why not?

_____

_____

_____

Day 7

1. What encouragement do you get from Psalm 100:4?

_____

_____

_____

2. A thankful heart can revolutionize the quality and enjoyment of your life. Do you agree? Why or why not?

_____

_____

_____

3. Read Psalm 28: 6-7. Instead of grumbling or complaining, what approach did David take?

_____

_____

_____

How did the approach impact his attitude?

_____

_____

_____

4. David Steindel-Rast said, "It's not joy that makes us grateful, but gratitude that makes us joyful." Do you agree? Why or why not?

_____

_____

_____

5. How would it impact your actions if you woke up tomorrow with only the things you thanked God for today?

_____

_____

_____

Week

9

Create an Obsession for Praying

Focal Verse

Never stop praying. (1 Thessalonians 5:17 CEV)

In June of 2013 news broadcasts across the country featured a little boy named Grayson Clamp doing something he had never done before. The three-year-old was born without the auditory nerves that carry sound to the brain. Attempts to restore his hearing with a cochlear implant were unsuccessful, so doctors at the University of North Carolina tried an experimental procedure to implant an auditory nerve directly into Grayson's brain. This procedure proved successful, and millions of people enjoyed seeing the look of wonder and joy on the little boy's face when he heard his father's voice for the first time.

Today, with the technology available communication is instant—but even then it is a delight to hear from a friend or family member who is far away. Just as we respond to those familiar voices with pleasure, God delights in hearing from His children.

Why do we pray? Certainly it is not to inform God of what we need. He already knows everything about our situation, and, far better than we could devise, He knows the answer that will be best for us. Prayer is meant in part to remind us of how dependent on God we truly are. But prayer is not just for our benefit. God enjoys hearing us pray! When we come to Him in faith and make our petitions before His throne of grace, His heart rejoices. He likes hearing our voices. Let us never go long without going to Him in prayer.

The sacrifice of the wicked is an abomination to the LORD: but the prayer of the upright is his delight. (Proverbs 15:8)

Questions for discussion, reflection and application

Day 1

1. According to 2 Corinthians 3:5, what is the source of your sufficiency? How can you access the source?

_____

_____

_____

2. Your prayer life is a reflection of knowing God, of which there are three levels:

   a. Acknowledgement - Recognizing that God exists

   b. Acquaintance – Familiar with, but not knowing Him well

   c. Adoration – Deep love and respect; worship

   Do you agree with these statements? Why or why not? Which level describes you best?

_____

_____

_____

3. How would you evaluate the quality and quantity of your current prayer life?

4. Do you pray as a last resort ("I've done all that I can do. The only thing left is to pray") or do you pray as a first resort? Why?

5. When you pray, do you spend more time asking for help or in saying thanks? Why?

Day 2

1. According to John 14:13, why does Jesus say He will do whatever we ask in His name?

2. Based on John 16:24

   a. Why have you not received?

_____

_____

_____

   b. What will be the result of asking and receiving?

_____

_____

_____

   c. What does it look like to have your joy full?

_____

_____

_____

3. You cannot have joy without an intimate fellowship with Jesus; you cannot have an intimate fellowship with Jesus without prayer. Do you agree? Why or why not?

_____

_____

_____

4. Based on John 14:13 and John 16:24, how is glorifying God connected to your joy?

_____

_____

_____

5. Based on John 15:7 - 8 how is God glorified when He gives us what we ask in Jesus' name?

_____

_____

_____

Day 3

1. If you viewed prayer as bringing glory to God and joy to you, how might your prayer life change?

_____

_____

_____

2. How does John 15:4, 5 portray your dependence on God?

_____

_____

_____

3. Does the combination of your dependence on God, your desire to glorify Him, and your desire to experience joy lead you to pray or less?

_____

_____

_____

4. Read Psalm 86:4. Do you ever pray for joy? Why or why not?

_____

_____

_____

5. Read Matthew 26:39-44

   a. What lessons can you learn from Jesus' prayer?

_____

_____

_____

   b. Can you incorporate those lessons into your prayer life?

_____

_____

_____

   c. Why or why not?

_____

_____

_____

Day 4

1. Read Mark 11:22-25. Name three conditions Jesus mentions for your prayers to be heard and answered.

_____

_____

_____

2. Read John 15:7. What does Jesus say must abide in you in order for your prayers to be heard and answered?

_____

_____

_____

3. Based on Matthew 6:5-9. What warning does Jesus give? What message do you think he is communicating?

_____

_____

_____

4. Since He is a loving father, why doesn't God always give you everything that you ask for?

_____

_____

_____

5. What does it say about you if you are too busy to pray?

_____

_____

_____

Day 5

1. Do you truly expect your prayers to be answered? Why or why not?

_____

_____

_____

2. 1 Thessalonians 5:17 says pray continually.

a. Do you find it challenging to endure in prayer, particularly when no answers are apparent? Why or why not?

_____

_____

_____

b. If you find it challenging, what steps have you found helpful in staying motivated?

_____

_____

_____

3. Even if you don't see an obvious answer to your prayers, do you believe God has answered? Why or why not?

_____

_____

_____

4. Read Philippians 4:6 - 7.

   a. What should you do rather than worry?

   _____

   _____

   _____

   b. What will result?

   _____

   _____

   _____

   c. Describe the characteristics of the result.

   _____

   _____

   _____

5. You can choose to worry or you can choose to pray. However, you cannot choose to do both at the same time. Do you agree? Why or why not?

_____

_____

_____

6. Based on Psalm 118:21 and Psalm 40:5, what should be your response to God's goodness?

_____

_____

_____

Day 6

1. When praying, many of us ask God to change our circumstances. However, based on Romans 8:29, God may be using our circumstances to change us. Do you agree? Why or why not?

_____

_____

_____

2. C.S Lewis said: "I pray because I can't help myself. I pray because I'm helpless. I pray because the need flows out of me all the time, waking and sleeping. It doesn't change God, it changes me." How does prayer change you?

_____

_____

_____

3. List the reasons the following verses say you should pray:

   a. Matthew 7:7

_____

_____

_____

   b. Matthew 26:41

_____

_____

_____

   c. Luke 18:1

_____

_____

_____

4. Read James 5:16.

   a. Does God hear and answer only the prayers of righteous people?

_____

_____

_____

b. Who is righteous? How does one become righteous?

_____

_____

_____

c. What is effective prayer?

_____

_____

_____

d. What is fervent prayer?

_____

_____

_____

Day 7

1. Read James 5:13 and fill in the blank. Is anyone among you suffering? Let him _____.

2. When you are having problems, do you:

   a. Pray more often

   b. Pray less often

   c. Pray with the same frequency as you did before the problem

   d. Abandon praying altogether

3. What is the common command in 1 Thessalonians 5:17 and Acts 6:4?

_____

_____

_____

4. How are you encouraged by Psalm 100?

_____

_____

_____

5. Read James 1:5-8. How does doubt impact your prayer life?

_____

_____

_____

6. In what ways do your prayers reflect an attitude of "My kingdom come" instead of "Your kingdom come"?

_____

_____

_____

Week

10

Develop an Eternal Perspective

Focal Verse

Set your mind on the things above, not on the things that are on earth. (Colossians 3:2 NASB)

Investment advisors often tell their clients to not be alarmed about short term ups and downs in the value of their portfolio. Instead, they should take a long term view. Likewise, we should not get discouraged when we have some short term problems, because if you believe God is in control and that in the long term you will benefit, you can have peace.

Pastor Duane Scott Willis and his wife Janet are great examples of keeping an eternal perspective.

They dearly loved the nine children God had given them. But at mid-morning on November 8, 1994, a fiery auto explosion on I-94 in Milwaukee claimed the lives of their six youngest children.

Eight day later, while, while still recovering from their burns, Pastor Scot and his wife held a press conference to address the media.

The following statements are excerpts from that news conference.

Their God—Their Praise

"Psalm 34 says, 'I will bless the Lord at all times: His praise shall continually be in my mouth. O, taste and see that the Lord is good.' Janet and I want to praise and thank God. There is no question in our minds that God is good, and we praise Him in all things. God is a great God."

Their Children—Their Pain

"We believe children are a heritage of the Lord. We thank God for six precious children: four rascally boys, a sweet girl, so much like her mother, and a little baby just beginning to smile and grow. We understood that they were given of the Lord, and we understood they weren't ours. They were His, and we were stewards of those children. And so God took them back. He is the Giver and Taker of life. We must tell you that we hurt and sorrow as you parents would for your children. The depth of pain is indescribable. The Bible expresses our feelings that we sorrow, but not as those without hope."

Their Confidence in God's Word

"What gives us our firm foundation for our hope is the Bible. The truth of God's Word assures us that Ben, Joe, Sam, Hank, Elizabeth, and Peter are in Heaven with Jesus Christ. We know, based upon the Word of God, where they are. Our strength rests in the

Word of God. The Bible is sure and gives us confidence. Everything God promises is true."

Their Preparation for this Moment

"We thank God for His preparation for this problem. Janet became a Christian as a teenager after reading a gospel tract that somebody had handed her. On February 5, 1975, I [Scott] trusted Jesus Christ as my Lord and Savior."

Questions for discussion, reflection and application

1. 1 Corinthians 15:19 (NIV) says: "If only for this life we have hope in Christ, we are of all people most to be pitied."

   a. How you hoped in Christ for this life only?

   _____

   _____

   _____

   b. How does the verse affect your view of problems?

   _____

   _____

   _____

2. Pastor Steven Cole said: "While we should enjoy the blessings God gives us in this life, we should hold those things loosely and instead focus on God and being in heaven with Him." Do you agree? Why or why not?

   _____

   _____

   _____

3. Read 1 Peter 2:11.

   a. What terms does he use to describe our current status?

   _____

   _____

   _____

   b. Explain the meaning of the terms.

   _____

   _____

   _____

   c. How do the terms impact your view of problems?

   _____

   _____

   _____

4. Does Philippians 3:20 support or contradict 1 Peter 2:11?

   _____

   _____

   _____

5. According to Luke 10:20, why should you rejoice?

   _____

   _____

   _____

Day 2

1. Instead of focusing on eternity, it is easy to get distracted and focus on the next milestone in our life.

   a. Identify a milestone on which you are focusing? Retirement, graduation, marriage, recovering from injury/illness

   _____

   _____

   _____

   b. Is the milestone preventing you from having an eternal perspective? How?

   _____

   _____

   _____

2. Read Hebrews 12:2. What does "for the joy that was set before him" mean?

   _____

   _____

   _____

3. Read 1 Peter 1:3-6

   a. According to verse 3 we have a living _____
   _____ through the _____
   _____ of Jesus.

b. Verse 4 says we have an inheritance. In your own words, describe the three characteristics of our inheritance?

_____

_____

_____

c. Read verse 6. What attitude should you have regarding your problems?

_____

_____

_____

d. Read verse 6. How does Peter describe the duration of your problems?

_____

_____

_____

Day 3

Read 2 Corinthians 4:16-18

1. What two adjectives does Paul use to describe the troubles he is facing?

_____

_____

_____

2. What benefits does he look forward to reaping as a result of enduring the current troubles?

_____

_____

_____

3. How does Paul describe the things we see versus the things we do see?

_____

_____

_____

4. As you go through various problems, what encouragement can you draw from these verses?

_____

_____

_____

Day 4

1. Identify a problem you are facing.

   a. How do you feel when you think about it from an earthly perspective?

_____

_____

_____

b. How do you act?

_____

_____

_____

c. How do you feel when you think about it from an eternal perspective?

_____

_____

_____

d. How do you act?

_____

_____

_____

e. What specific steps can you take to develop and sustain an eternal perspective regarding the problem?

_____

_____

_____

2. What encouragement can you draw from Romans 8:18 and 2 Corinthians 4:16-18?

_____

_____

_____

Day 5

1. In Revelation 21:1-4, John describes our eternal reality. What impact does it have when you are in the midst of problems?

_____

_____

_____

2. Romans 8:17. What does it mean to be co-heirs with Christ?

_____

_____

_____

3. Psalm 51:12 says restore to me the joy of your salvation? What was your level of joy at the time you were saved? Does reflecting on that time and looking ahead help you recapture that joy, even in the midst of problems? Why or why not?

_____

_____

_____

Day 6

1. Hebrews 2:15 says that many people live in "slavery" to the fear of death. Do you live in fear of death? Why or why not?

_____

_____

_____

2. Read Philippians 1:21. How did Paul view death?

_____

_____

_____

3. In John 16:20-22 Jesus talks about the pain of childbirth.

   a. What makes women willing to endure the pain?

_____

_____

_____

   b. What implications does it hold for your willingness to endure problems?

_____

_____

_____

4. Martin Luther said: "I have but two days in my calendar - Today, and the Day I stand before Christ." He recognized that every day of this life is preparation for the day when we will stand before God in eternity. We have a choice: we can view life through God's perspective or we can simply view life through the world's perspective. The choice we make will greatly affect our thinking and actions. Which way do you view life?

_____

_____

_____

5. A great way to determine how you view life is to complete this sentence:

I want Jesus to return, BUT...

_____

_____

_____

Fill in the blank: I want spend more time with my grandchildren, I want to retire, I want to travel, I want to live to be 100, I want to complete by "Bucket List", etc.

6. C.S. Lewis said 'If you read history you will find that the Christians who did the most for the present world were precisely those who thought the most of the next. It is since Christians have largely ceased to think of the other world that they have become so ineffective in this."

Do you agree? Why or why not?

_____

_____

_____

Day 7

1. Read James 4:14. How does the verse impact your view of life on this planet and problems you may experience?

_____

_____

_____

2. 2. What encouragement do you get from the lyrics of When We All Get Heaven?

> When we all get to heaven,
>
> what a day of rejoicing that will be!
>
> When we all see Jesus,
>
> we'll sing and shout the victory.

_____

_____

_____

3. In 2 Corinthians 5:4 Paul says we "groan while we are in this tent, burdened as we are".

We groan because we are in this imperfect reality, in these early bodies (tents) and we look forward to the time when that reality is replaced with the glories of Heaven. Do you agree? Why or why not?

_____

_____

_____

4. Chuck Swindoll said: "Joy springs from viewing the day's events from eternity's perspective." Do you view the day's events that way? Why or why not?

_____

_____

_____

5. God loves me so much He sent His son to die for my sins, thus insuring that I will spend an eternity with Him. Because of that I will joyfully endure any difficult circumstances during the few years I am on this earth. Are those your sentiments? Why or why not?

_____

_____

_____

Week

11

Use Paul as a Role Model

Focal Verse

You must follow my example, as I follow the example of Christ.
(1 Corinthians 11:1 CEV)

A role model is a person others see as an example to be imitated. As Jesus promised, we will have many troubles in this world, so it is helpful to imitate someone who has handled difficult times.

Paul records some of his difficulties in 2 Corinthians 11:24-27. Those difficulties include:

» Being beaten with belts and rods, pelted with stones, shipwrecked, jailed

» Being cold, hungry, thirsty, naked, sleep-deprived

» Experiencing health problems and running for his life

Paul's response to his troubles: For our present troubles are small and won't last very long. Yet they produce for us a glory that vastly outweighs them and will last forever! So we don't look at the troubles we can see now; rather, we fix our gaze on things that cannot be seen. For the things we see now will soon be gone, but the things we cannot see will last forever. (2 Corinthians 4:17-4:18 NLT)

Questions for reflection, discussion and application

Day 1

1. Read Philippians 3:1 and 4:4. Remember, Paul was in prison when he wrote this letter.

   a. What does Paul command the Philippians to do?

   _____

   _____

   _____

   b. What does it mean to rejoice in the Lord?

   _____

   _____

   _____

   c. Is possible to rejoice in the midst of problems? Why or why not?

   _____

   _____

   _____

2. Read 2 Corinthians 6:10.

a. Is it possible to have sorrow and rejoice at the same time?

_____

_____

_____

b. Did Paul experience these emotions at the same time?

_____

_____

_____

c. Have you experienced these emotions at the same time? When? What were the circumstances?

_____

_____

_____

3. Read 2 Corinthians 12:7-10.

a. What was Paul's first response to health problems? (v.8)

_____

_____

_____

b. How did God respond to Paul's plea? (v.9a)

_____

_____

_____

c. What was Paul's second response to his health problem? (v.9b, 10)

_____

_____

_____

d. What can you learn from Paul' responses?

_____

_____

_____

4. Read Acts 20:17 - 24.

a. Did Paul have a mission?

_____

_____

_____

b. Did he encounter difficulties in carrying out his mission?

_____

_____

_____

c. What is your mission?

_____

_____

_____

Day 2

1. According to Philippians 1:12-14:

   a. What did Paul see as the benefits of his imprisonment?

   _____

   _____

   _____

   b. What caused him to conclude that his imprisonment offered benefits?

   _____

   _____

   _____

2. Based on Philippians 4:11-13, 19:

   a. What was Paul's response to scarcity? (v.11)

   _____

   _____

   _____

   b. Based on verse 11, do you think Paul had always had that attitude toward scarcity? Why or why not?

   _____

   _____

   _____

c. What was Paul's secret of being content in every situation? (v13)

_____

_____

_____

d. Based on verse 19, God's resources to meet your needs will never expire. Do you agree? Why or why not?

_____

_____

_____

e. How do you typically respond to scarcity?

_____

_____

_____

f. How may your response change as a result of imitating Paul?

_____

_____

_____

Day 3

1. Read Philippians 1:21.

    a. How did Paul view his death?

    _____

    _____

    _____

    b. Explain "To live is Christ, to die is gain."

    _____

    _____

    _____

2. According to Philippians 2:15

    a. When do Christians "shine as lights in the world"?

    _____

    _____

    _____

    b. How are you being a light in the world?

    _____

    _____

    _____

3. In your own words define "worry".

_____

_____

_____

4. What did you worry about this week?

_____

_____

_____

5. Is it possible not to worry? Why or why not?

_____

_____

_____

Day 4

1. More Christians are addicted to worry than to all the other addictions combined. Do you agree? Why or why not?

_____

_____

_____

2. When you worry, you are saying that your problems are bigger than God's promises. Do you agree? Why or why not?

_____

_____

_____

3. According to Matthew 6:30 what is the underlying cause for worry?

_____

_____

_____

4. You can either pray or worry, but you can't pray and worry because the two cannot coexist at the same time. Do you agree? Why or why not?

_____

_____

_____

5. What does Paul mean in Philippians 4:5 when he says "The Lord is near?"

_____

_____

_____

Day 5

Read Philippians 4:6-7

a. The antidote for anxiety is "worry about nothing and pray about everything." Do you agree? Why or why not?

_____

_____

_____

b. Does "Be anxious for nothing" include problems?

_____

_____

_____

c. Fill in the blank. According to Philippians 4:7 when we pray we experience the _____ of God.

d. What are the two truths about the peace of God? (Phil 4:7)

_____

_____

_____

e. What is the meaning of "Guard your hearts and minds"?

_____

_____

_____

f. Why do you think prayerful dependence upon God brings about peace when facing difficult circumstances?

_____

_____

_____

g. Have you experienced the peace of God and the God of peace after praying in the midst of difficult circumstances? If so, what was the situation? What happened after you prayed?

_____

_____

_____

h. Do you think most of God's people experience God's peace? Why or why not?

_____

_____

_____

1. Philippians 3:17-21, Paul says that you are to follow the example of him and others who eagerly await Jesus' return, not those whose mind is on earthly things.

a. How are your values being shaped by knowing that this world is not all there is and that your true citizenship is in Heaven?

_____

_____

_____

b. How does that knowledge and those values impact:

» The way in which you live your life?

_____

_____

_____

» Your ability to rejoice during difficult circumstances?

_____

_____

_____

2. Despite all of his difficulties, according to 2 Corinthians 7:4, what was Paul's overall attitude?

_____

_____

_____

Can you make the same claim when you are facing difficulties? Why or why not?

_____

_____

_____

3. Read 2 Corinthians 1:8-10.

   a. What does Paul see as a benefit of his difficulties? (v.9)

_____

_____

_____

   b. Do you see the same benefit when you face difficult circumstances? Why or why not?

_____

_____

_____

4. Read 2 Corinthians 4:17.

   a. What two words did Paul use to describe his difficulties? (v.17)

_____

_____

_____

   b. How was he able to have that attitude? (v.17)

_____

_____

_____

c. How did he describe the things he saw to things he did not see?

_____

_____

_____

d. How often do you display a similar attitude when facing difficult circumstances?

_____

_____

_____

5. Read Romans 8:18. Can you make the same claim? Does this verse support or contradict 2 Corinthians 4:17?

_____

_____

_____

Day 7

1. In Romans 12:2, Paul says renew your mind. In your own words, describe what this means.

_____

_____

_____

2. In Philippians 4: 8 Paul mentioned eight characteristics that our thoughts should have. Define what you think each characteristic means.

a.

_____

_____

_____

b.

_____

_____

_____

c.

_____

_____

_____

d.

_____

_____

_____

e.

_____

_____

_____

f.

_____

_____

_____

g.

_____

_____

_____

h.

_____

_____

_____

3. Which characteristic do you meet most often? Why?

_____

_____

_____

4. Which characteristic do you struggle to meet? Why?

_____

_____

_____

5. How have you seen God grow you in that area?

_____

_____

_____

Week

12

Serve Others

Focal Verse

*For, dear brothers, you have been given freedom:
not freedom to do wrong, but freedom to love
and serve each other. (Galatians 5:13TLB)*

When we are in the midst of problems, our tendency is to focus on ourselves. Bob and Barbara Malizzo chose a different path.

Their daughter, Michelle Malizzo Ballog, went into the University of Illinois Medical Center at Chicago to have surgery to replace a temporary stent in her liver.

She never woke up from the surgery.

Monitoring errors were made while she was under anesthesia, and Michelle, whose youngest daughter had turned one year old the day before, stopped breathing and suffered cardiac arrest on the operating room table. She lapsed into a coma and died nine days later at age 39.

Her parents and sister had no idea that Michelle's death had been caused by preventable medical errors, of which the monitoring problem was only the first. When they found out, they were livid. Bob remembers angrily asking doctors: "How could this happen?"

To the family's astonishment, hospital officials did not duck their questions, cover up their mistakes or hide behind lawyers. Instead, they shared the tragic details.

As a result, Bob and Barbara made a couple of surprising decisions of their own: 1) They chose not to sue and, 2) they joined the hospital's safety review committee to help prevent future errors.

In their role as lay members of the committee, Bob, Barbara, and their daughter Kristina Chavez hear about medical errors and "near-misses" that occur at the University of Illinois Medical Center at Chicago and other hospitals. They offer a unique perspective that is often lacking in these types of meetings. Their recommendations have led to the implementation of several procedural changes.

Bob and Barb explained the family's thinking in joining the panel: "We might be able to save someone's life."

Questions for discussion, reflection and application

Day 1

1. Read Mark 10:45.

a. How did Jesus describe His mission?

_____

_____

_____

b. What implication does Jesus' stated mission have for us?

_____

_____

_____

2. Read Mark 9:34 – 35.

a. Why were the disciples arguing?

_____

_____

_____

b. How does the disciples' view of greatness match the world's view today?

_____

_____

_____

c. What was Jesus' response to their argument?

_____

_____

_____

3. Read Matthew 20:27-28. How does it support or contradict Mark 9:34.

_____

_____

_____

4. Read John 13:5, 12-17. How did Jesus serve His disciples? What was Jesus' point in serving them this way?

_____

_____

_____

5. Read Philippians 2:5-8. How do these verses support or contradict John 13:5?

_____

_____

_____

Day 2

1. Based on Ephesians 2:10, why were we created?

_____

_____

_____

2. According to Colossians 3:23 – 24 and Ephesians 2:10, whenever you serve others in any way, you are actually serving God and fulfilling your purpose. Do you agree? Why or why not?

_____

_____

_____

3. Based on Genesis 45:1-7, what was the purpose for which God used Joseph's service?

_____

_____

_____

4. Read Romans 15:1. What are the two commands? What obstacles might you encounter in carrying out these commands?

_____

_____

_____

Day 3

1. James 2:17 says faith without works is dead. Is service an indication of faith? Why or why not?

_____

_____

_____

2. Read 1 Peter 4:11.

   a. What is the source of your ability to serve others?

_____

_____

_____

   b. Who should get the credit when you serve others?

_____

_____

_____

3. What are your spiritual gifts?

   a. How have you used those gifts to serve others?

_____

_____

_____

b. How did you feel when you used those gifts to serve others?

_____

_____

_____

c. How might you us those gifts to serve others, even if you are in the midst of a problem?

_____

_____

_____

4. One of the beauties of serving others is that it requires no spiritual gifts. Do you agree? Why or why not? How might you serve others in ways that do not require spiritual gifts?

_____

_____

_____

5. What is the message Jesus is communicating in Matthew 6:3?

_____

_____

_____

How does the message apply today as you serve others?

_____

_____

_____

Day 4

1. Richard Foster said: "Nothing disciplines the inordinate desires of the flesh like service, and nothing transforms the desires of the flesh like serving in hiddenness. The flesh whines against service but screams against hidden service. It strains and pulls for honor and recognition. It will devise subtle, religiously acceptable means to call attention to the service rendered. If we stoutly refuse to give in to this lust of the flesh, we crucify it. Every time we crucify the flesh, we crucify our pride and arrogance."

   Do you agree? Why or why not?

   _____

   _____

   _____

2. Based on Matthew 5:16, should you seek recognition for service? Why or why not?

   _____

   _____

   _____

3. Read Matthew 6:4. What does the verse tell us about rewards for serving?

   _____

   _____

   _____

4. According to Proverbs 11:25, what can you expect as a result of serving others?

_____

_____

_____

5. When most people are facing problems, they are usually inclined to:

   a. Blame others

   b. Hold a pity party

   c. Withdraw

   d. Serve others

   e. Circle all that apply

Day 5

1. Why might it be easier to justify selfishness in the midst of suffering?

_____

_____

_____

2. In what ways may you be a more effective ambassador of the gospel in the midst of suffering?

_____

_____

_____

3. How does the presence of God enable you to minister to others and put their needs above your own?

_____

_____

_____

4. When facing problems, do you serve others less, more or about the same? Why?

_____

_____

_____

5. Who is a model of service that has impacted you? What makes that person a role model?

_____

_____

_____

Day 6

1. Have you served others when you were going through difficulties? Describe the circumstance. How did you serve? What was the outcome? How did you feel afterwards?

_____

_____

_____

2. Read Philippians 1:12. Even though Paul was in prison awaiting execution, he had joy because his focus was not on himself but on serving God by furthering the gospel. Do you agree? Why or why not?

_____

_____

_____

3. According to Philippians 1:3- 4, what was one way that Paul served others while he was in prison?

_____

_____

_____

4. Have you prayed for someone even as you were experiencing difficulty?

_____

_____

_____

5. How can the following sample prayer from Jack Watts help as you serve others?

_____

_____

_____

Father,

Allow me to serve others with a joyful heart; never keeping score;

Always giving; never expecting to receive.

Allow me to give of myself, to give of my talents and of my goods,

To give of my time and of my energy, to give of my heart and of my soul.

Help me understand the needs of others, never criticizing, never demeaning,

Never scolding, never condemning.

You have been so gracious to me, always loving, always forgiving,

Always restoring; never gloating over my defeats, even when I have been so wrong.

Father, keep a condemning spirit far from my heart and further from my lips.

Allow me to serve others as you serve, with gentleness, compassion, and tenderness, never diminishing the worth of another, choosing to extend mercy to the brokenhearted, like you have repeatedly shown it to me. Amen.

Day 7

1. Pastor Rick Warren said: "Don't waste your pain. Use it to help others."

Candace Lightner's 13- year-old daughter, Cari, was killed by a drunk driver. Four days after Cari's death, Candace started up a grassroots organization to advocate for stiffer penalties for drunk driving. She quit her job and used her savings to fund Mothers against Drunk Drivers (MADD).

Today, there is at least one MADD office in every state of the United States and at least one in each province of Canada. These offices offer victim services and many resources involving alcohol safety. MADD has shown that drunk driving has been reduced by half since its founding.

Steve Gallison lost his job. While unemployed, he sharpened her skills as a trainer and began a new career. He eventually became director of an outplacement center. To date, the organization has helped more than 200,000 professional, technical and administrative professionals get jobs.

Suzy Brown's husband divorced her after 33 years. In 2007, while still going through her divorce, she started RADiCAL, which stands for: Rising Above Divorce In Confidence And Love. The purpose of the 10-week support group and course is to empower midlife women who are struggling with a divorce to get unstuck and move on and be the woman they were created to be.

Do you think Candace, Steve and Suzy wasted their pain or used it to help others? Why or why not?

_____

_____

_____

2. What is your reaction to John Wesley's advice?

_____

_____

_____

Do all the good you can, by all the means you can, in all the ways you can, In all the places you can, at all the times you can, for all the people you can, as long as ever you can.

3. According to Psalm 100.2, what should our attitude be when serving? Do you have that attitude when you serve? Why or why not?

_____

_____

_____

4. How are you currently serving others?

_____

_____

_____

5. Make a list of specific people. Identify a need they may have and how you might serve them this week.

   a. Spouse

   b. Family

   c. Children

   d. Neighbor

   e. Fellow believers

6. Anne Frank said: "No one has ever become poor by giving." Do you agree? Why or why not?

   _____

   _____

   _____

7. What encouragement can you draw from Galatians 6:9?

   _____

   _____

   _____

Week

13

Keep Your Eyes Fixed on Jesus

Focal Verse

Let us fix our eyes on Jesus, the author and perfecter of our faith, who for the joy set before him endured the cross, scorning its shame, and sat down at the right hand of the throne of God.
(Hebrews 12:2)

In dog obedience training, they put a dog at one end of a room and its master at the other end of the room, with a plate of food in the middle. And then the master calls the dog. If the dog eyes the food, he's a goner; he'll go straight for it. So they teach the dog to focus his eyes on the master. If he keeps his eyes on the master, he won't be tempted. Instead of heading for the food, he'll head straight to the master. Likewise, we need to keep our eyes on our Master. Otherwise, we can get distracted, not by food but by life's inevitable problems.

Questions for discussion, reflection and application

Day 1

1. "Fixed" means concentrating our gaze; to look away from other things in order to focus all of our attention on one thing.

   Fixing your eyes on Jesus means that when the inevitable problems come, instead of starting with your circumstances and then trying to find Jesus, you start with Jesus and view your circumstances through His eyes. Do you agree? Why or why not?

   _____

   _____

   _____

2. What encouragement can you draw from this popular song by Helen Howarth Lemmel?

   _____

   _____

   _____

Turn Your Eyes upon Jesus

Turn your eyes upon Jesus, Look full in His wonderful face and the things of Earth will grow strangely dim, In the light of His glory and grace

3. Read Philippians 3:1 and 4:4. Why does Paul say "Rejoice in the Lord" instead of "Rejoice in your circumstances?"

_____

_____

_____

4. Read Philippians 3:13. What does Paul mean by "reaching forward to those things which are ahead?" How can doing so help you rejoice when facing a problem?

_____

_____

_____

Day 2

1. Jesus trusted His Father from beginning to end in his earthly ministry. Do you agree? Why or why not? Should you emulate that approach? How will doing so help us in times of problems?

_____

_____

_____

2. Read Matthew 14:14 - 20. The disciples had seen Jesus heal a leper, heal a centurion's servant, heal Peter's mother-in-law, calm the winds and the sea, cast out demons, and raise a girl from the dead and they had seen him heal several of the sick

among the multitude. Yet, after surveying the huge number of people, they recommended that Jesus send them away so they could buy themselves some food.

Were the disciples focusing on the circumstances or on Jesus? Why do you say that? Do you usually focus on your circumstances or Jesus?

_____

_____

_____

3. Read Hebrews 12:1.

   a. What is the meaning of "the race that is set before us"?

   _____

   _____

   _____

   b. How does Jesus' example help you "run with endurance"?

   _____

   _____

   _____

4. How does obeying Philippians 4:6 help you fix your eyes on Jesus?

   _____

   _____

   _____

Day 3

1. Based on 1 Thessalonians 5:17, will praying about a circumstance one time help you keep focus on Jesus? Why or why not?

_____

_____

_____

2. Philippians 4:8 provides a grid through which we should run our thoughts. How does doing so help you keep your eyes fixed on Jesus?

_____

_____

_____

3. Based on James 1:22, is it enough simply to know the things you should do to keep your eyes fixed on Jesus? Why or why not?

_____

_____

_____

4. What is the common message of 2 Peter 3:13 and Colossians 3:2? How does that message help you fix your eyes on Jesus when you have problems?

_____

_____

_____

Day 4

1. According to Luke 22:69, Jesus is seated at the right hand of God. According to 1 John 2: 1, Jesus is our advocate. Contemplate that image for a moment. As your advocate and given His lofty position, what kinds of things do you think Jesus is doing to benefit you? How does the thought of His doing that enable you to rejoice when you have problems?

_____

_____

_____

2. In John 1:32-34, John proclaimed that Jesus was the Messiah. In Matthew 11:1- 3, John sent two disciples to ask Jesus if he, in fact, was the Messiah. What caused John to start to doubt that Jesus was who He said was? What causes you to start to doubt?

_____

_____

_____

3. How would your focus on Jesus be impacted if you rehearsed meeting him and hearing Him say to you, "Well done, good and faithful servant. You have been faithful over a little; I will set you over much. Enter into the joy of your master." (Matthew 25:21)

_____

_____

_____

4. Read Hebrews 12:1-3.

a. What does it mean that Jesus is the "author" and "perfector" of our faith?

_____

_____

_____

b. What was the joy set before him?

_____

_____

_____

c. Did Jesus enjoy the cross?

_____

_____

_____

d. How does what Jesus endured help you face your problems and not grow weary?

_____

_____

_____

Day 5

1. Forgetfulness can cause us to take our eyes off Jesus. How does Psalm 77:11 encourage you?

_____

_____

_____

List 3 things Jesus has done for you.

_____

_____

_____

2. During times of problems it is helpful to:

a. Remember who God is. Read Genesis1:1 and Exodus 3:6 and fill in the blanks.

» He is the _____ of the heavens and the earth.

» He is the God of _____ , _____ ,
and _____

b. Remember God's power. According to Isaiah 46:9-10, what power does God have?

_____

_____

_____

c. c. Remember God's love for you. Based on Romans 5:8, how much does God love you?

_____

_____

_____

d. Remember God's promises. What promises does God give you in Deuteronomy 31:6 and Philippians 4:19?

_____

_____

_____

e. Remember your status with God. Based on Romans 8:17:

» What is your status?

_____

_____

_____

» What is the benefit of that status when you are facing a problem?

_____

_____

_____

   f. Remember your destination. According to Philippians 3:20, where is your citizenship?

_____

_____

_____

3. Think back over your life. When was the last time God did not bring you through a problem?

_____

_____

_____

Day 6

1. Read Psalm 16:8.

   a. Where has the Psalmist set the Lord?

_____

_____

_____

b. What is the result?

_____

_____

_____

c. Have you taken the same steps as the Psalmist? Why or why not?

_____

_____

_____

2. C. H. Spurgeon said:

"I can bear witness that whenever I am in deeps of sorrow, nothing will do for me but 'Jesus only.' . . . I retreat to the innermost citadel of our holy faith, namely, to the very heart of Christ, when my spirit is assailed by temptation, or besieged with sorrow and anguish.

What is more, my witness is that whenever I have high spiritual enjoyments, rich enjoyments, they are always connected with Jesus only. . . The sublimest, the most inebriating, the most divine of all joys, must be found in Jesus only. . . I find if I want to labor much, I must live on Jesus only; if I desire to suffer patiently, I must feed on Jesus only; if I wish to wrestle with God successfully, I must plead Jesus only; if I aspire to conquer sin, I must use the blood of Jesus only; if I pant to learn the mysteries of heaven, I must seek the teachings of Jesus only. I believe that anything which we add to Christ lowers our position, and that the more elevated our soul becomes, the more nearly like what it is to be when it shall enter into the region of the perfect, the more completely everything else will sink, die out, and Jesus, Jesus, Jesus only, will be the first and the last."

How close are you to matching his perspective?

_____

_____

_____

3. T. E. Marsh wrote on the fullness that is in Christ Jesus:

» In Christ there is full acceptance, therefore do not doubt Him.

» In Christ there is peace, therefore trust Him.

» In Christ there is life, therefore abide in Him.

» In Christ there is blessing, therefore delight in Him.

» In Christ there is light, therefore follow Him.

» In Christ there is power, therefore wait on Him.

» In Christ there is all truth, therefore learn from Him.

» In Christ there is grace, therefore receive from Him.

» In Christ there is joy, therefore rejoice in Him.

» In Christ there is unlimited wealth, therefore depend on Him.

» In Christ there is strength, therefore lean on Him.

Do you agree? Why or why not?

_____

_____

_____

4. No matter how serious your problem, the worst that it can do on this earth is to kill you. Through His death and resurrection, Jesus has conquered that enemy. Do you share this perspective? Why or why not?

_____

_____

_____

Day 7

1. Read Matthew 14:24 - 32

   a. What was Peter able to do supernaturally? (v.29)

_____

_____

_____

   b. Why was he able to do it? (v.29)

_____

_____

_____

   c. What did he start looking at instead of Jesus? (v.30)

_____

_____

_____

d. What emotion did Peter feel? (v.30)

_____

_____

_____

e. What happened once he took his eyes off Jesus? (v.30)

_____

_____

_____

f. In what areas of your life are you, like Peter, focusing on your circumstances instead of Jesus?

_____

_____

_____

g. What emotion are you feeling?

_____

_____

_____

2. Based on Isaiah 26:3 what emotion results from keeping your eyes on Jesus? Have you experienced this emotion during problems? Describe the circumstance.

_____

_____

_____

3. Finish this sentence: Because I have fixed my eyes on Jesus, I can....

a.

_____

_____

_____

b.

_____

_____

_____

c.

_____

_____

_____